the Kampung boy

the Kampung boy

Lat

Berita
Publishing Sdn Bhd (15654-K)

BERITA PUBLISHING SDN. BHD. (15654-K)
No. 16-20, Jalan 4/109E
Desa Business Park, Taman Desa
Off Jalan Klang Lama
58100 KUALA LUMPUR
MALAYSIA

Tel: 603-76208111 Fax: 603-76208018
E-mail: newproduct@beritapub.com.my

A member of Malaysian Book Publishers Association
Membership No. 198105

ISBN 967-969-410-0

First published 1979
Second reprint 1981
Tenth reprint 2002
Eleventh reprint 2003

Printed by
Sanon Printing Corporation Sdn. Bhd.
No. 5, 7 & 9, Jalan 10/108C
Taman Sungai Besi
57100 KUALA LUMPUR

Dedicated to my mum, Cik Norazian and dad, Mohd. Khalid.

I cannot truly recall, of course, what happened in the first few years of my life. It was not until I had learnt to speak and been able to conduct conversations with my mother that I found out about my early days.

I was born in a kampung in the heart of the world's largest tin mining district — the Kinta Valley in Perak.

According to my mother, I was born at about ten o'clock in a Monday morning in our house. The task of delivering me into this world fell on my own grandmother. She had been the official midwife in the kampung for many years. I was mum's first child. My father's memory of this day was also quite clear. According to him, he was at that time under the house waiting anxiously when my grandmother called:

"Come and cradle your son!"

Minutes later dad was standing in the anjung (lounge) with me in his arms. Then he whispered the bilal's call softly in my ears just as any good Muslim father would do to his newly-born child.

Three days later dad paid
my grandmother $15
(normal charge for the first baby.)

Dad also presented my grandmother with the following items:

A roast chicken
A plate of yellow rice
A batik sarung.
These gifts were just a formality.

On the 45th day, the day of my mother's complete recovery from her "pantang" (taboo) period, I underwent some formalities myself. It was the "adat cukur kepala" (my hair-shaving ceremony.) Quite an affair, I must say. Dad invited neighbours and relatives. It was on this day that, just as the sun was rising, I was brought out of the house for the first time to feel the air outside.

The first part of this ceremony was of course the shaving. Grandma (who else?) did it. Then, bald and naked, I was carried to the front yard where, witnessed by more than a dozen well-wishers, she gave me a bath.

They dressed me in the finest clothings and put me in a hammock in which I had never been before. I must have felt very comfortable. Just as the hammock was swaying slowly, a group of the guests began chanting the sacred lyrics of the "Marhaban" (a song about the Prophet.)

Before long I dozed off.
Then the gathering adjourned
to some refreshments
my folks had for them.

And so life began
with a mother's love...

Oh! How affectionately and tenderly
mum cared for me. Everyday she
would wrap up my whole body in
the swaddling clothes...

Then she'd stuff
me with porridge

As I grew bigger, I learned to crawl.
By this time I had already started showing my main
physical features as an individual. I had a full round face
and although the bridge of my nose was quite low I had
no complaints because, as I discovered later, none of my
ancestors had a high nose bridge.

However, mum's description of my looks was rather
vague and unsatisfying. She said I looked sweet whenever
I smiled but on the whole I was by no means a beauty.

Yes, I would crawl all round the house all day long.
Sometimes I'd play with the spots of sunlight that fell on
the floor.

This is the split-level back portion of our house where I spent most of my time. On the lower level is the kitchen. Mum did her cooking on that table.

It was also in the kitchen that mum bathed me since I was too young to go to the river.

From the window in the front part of the house I
could see a rubber estate.
It was from the direction of this estate that a distant
roaring sound came and never seemed to stop.
It was the sound of a tin dredge, of course, about
which I shall tell you more later in this book.

I loved to look out of the window because that was
the nearest I could get to the surroundings outside the
house. I was not allowed to step out.

Sometimes I stuck my head out too far...

mum's bike

A cross-section of our house. It was made of "Cengai" wood. The chengai tree gives a very handsome timber that really lasts long.

At the age of four...

appiness was seeing aunt Khatijah, rubber small-holder, coming back om her daily tapping late in the morning.

I always offered her a helping hand in processing the "milk of the rubber tree." First, she'd add some liquid (later I discovered it was formic acid) into the latex and we'd stir it.

Then we'd wait for about 15 minutes or so for the latex to harden.

After that I'd help her flatten the coagulated rubber...

Then it went to the rollers
to be turned into sheets.
But usually by this time
I had to leave because mum
would be calling me back.

The reason mum called was either for me to eat or take care of my sister. Oh! yes, our family had already been bestowed with another member then — my sister, Maimunah.

I had always been curious about the tin dredge which kept on roaring from the other side of the plantation. One morning I broke one of mum's rules by sneaking out of the house compound.

What I saw was a huge thing
floating in the big pool of mud.
It was certainly huge for even
at a distance it looked very big.
No wonder it sounded so loud.
It would roar and once in a while
groan frighteningly...

like a monster!

Well... that was also the day I discovered how fierce mum could get.

I was so afraid of what mum would do to me that I was running like a barking deer! She lost me near Pak Alang's house when the man, who knew me by sight, showed sympathy for me...

But of course I got the thrashing later anyway.

My father was different.
He was a funny fellow. My sister and I would look forward to seeing him coming back from work in the afternoon. He was a government clerk in Batu Crajah.

He was a big man.

This was what he'd do first...

Then it was tea time for us. Usually we'd either have fried bananas or fried tapioca. Or boiled bananas ... or ... boiled tapioca. But occasionally mum would bake our favourite cake — kueh bengkang.

Mum baked kueh bengkang like this fire on top and below because we didn't have an oven. It is hemispherical in shape and made of rice flour, coconut milk, egg and palm sugar. Very tasty.

HEE!HEE!
HEE!HÊ!

MMMMMM...

... scratch his back.

Then we'd fool around with dad.
As you can see he was a very playful person

Just before sundown it was bath time.
This was another time we looked forward to:
when dad would take us to the river
not far behind the house.

On the way, we often stopped to look at
the weaverbirds' nests that hung high
on top of the bamboo trees.
I remember dad telling us an astonishing fact
about the weavers.

"These birds are very clever," he said.
"When the time comes for mama weaver
to lay eggs, papa weaver will do anything
to make her comfortable.
He will catch a firefly at night
and take it back to light up
their home."

Dad knew a lot about
such things.

At the river dad would always
try to impress us with his
diving stunts. He could do several
different styles...

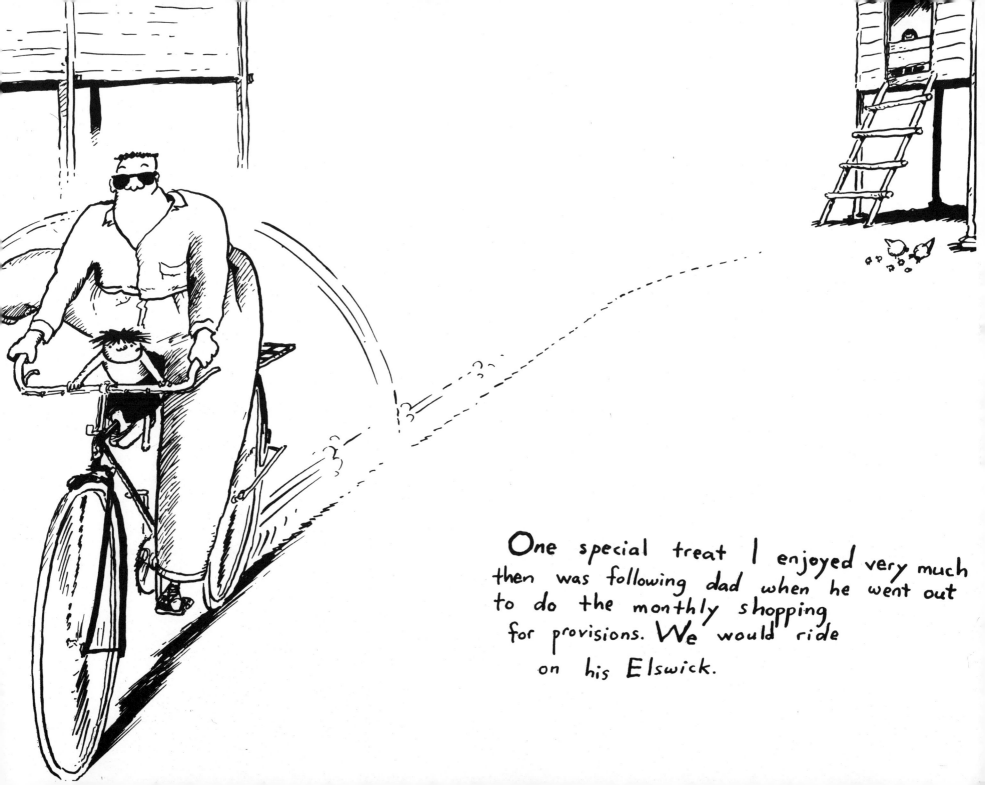

One special treat I enjoyed very much then was following dad when he went out to do the monthly shopping for provisions. We would ride on his Elswick.

...we had to give way.

As you can see our kampung lane was very narrow. Very rarely could we see a motor-car passing by. But when we saw one...

government
dispensary

dresse

This is our town.
Next to the dispensary on the left is Ah Yew's shop where we
do our shopping and next to his shop is a cloth dealer who is also a small-time goldsmit
On the extreme right is an Indian eating shop, next comes a book shop,
a rubber dealer and a bicycle shop.

We also never failed to wait
for the 5 o'clock mail train.
I loved looking at trains.

When the shopping was done
...would proceed to a tea stall
...front of the village mosque.
...ere the kampung men met and had
...ng conversations over coffee and tea.

...would share tea with dad who
...ould join in the talk. However,
...could not follow their
conversations. Needless to say,
I was there just to accompany
dad.

As I reached six years of age, when education became the task of my father, I was sent to Tuan Syed Ahmad's Koran reading class at the religious teacher's home. It was a must for children of my age to begin learning Tajwid (the art of reading Arabic with the correct enunciation) so that we could master the Koran.

Although it was my earliest stage of a formal education, I must admit that I was not very happy to see Tuan Syed for the first time that afternoon.

y enrolment in the class was made in the
ditional way. I can still remember clearly what
ppened. Dad handed over to Tuan Syed a bowl
glutinous rice, a fee of $1 and a small cane and
n said: "Tuan, I am handing over my son to
u in the hope that you'd teach him the Koran.
ake him as if he is your own child ... if he is
bborn or naughty don't hesitate to punish him
th this cane — as long as it doesn't reach the
ent of breaking any of his bones or blinding his
s." Tuan Syed took the cane and nodded.
us end the formality.
t I noticed the teacher already had his own
ne.

Tuan Syed was very particular about pronunciation.

And we were supposed to pronounce .....exactly...as... the... Arabs do...

One thing I discovered about an afternoon class was you tend to get sleepy

Before long I had already become used to the scene and had made acquaintance with some of the fellows. At the end of each month we'd pay the teacher for his service. Tuan Syed accepted any form of payment. Some of us would give him $1, some gave 50 cents, others gave him a plate of rice or sugar.

Or we could be like these three brothers here (the children of Meor Yusoff) who gave teacher firewood they picked on their way to class.

Even that was all right.

ese children of Meor Yusoff were in fact the first
nds that I made. I was rather afraid of them at
t because the way they talked and move around
ld lead you to branding them as the rough type.
t I admired them for their knowledge in fishing
ich seemed to be the most important thing in their
es.

ey always had interesting things to tell about the
er and fishing and many a time they invited me
come along and watch them inspect their fish
ps. But I would turn down their invitation because
vas not sure whether I was brave enough to go
the far-away and remote parts of the river.

t Meor Din, the eldest of the Meor brothers
ould say to me each time before we parted: "If you
ant to know the best spots for swimming and if you
ant to learn fishing, follow us."

ne day I just couldn't resist.

It was the most enjoyable afternoon for me as we inspected the fish traps. I felt I was very lucky because these chaps had invited me to join them. I was certain this friendship would turn out to be very important to the path of my life thereafter.

I had so much to learn. I couldn't swim and I didn't know how to handle a fish and I thought it was up to these fellows to teach me.
I was extremely proud to be with them.

walked back on a different route. As
were passing a swampy area, Meor Din
ted at some strange-looking plants I had
er seen before.

"hat do you think those are?" he asked.
id, "I don't know." "Those are monkey
," he said.

ey were pitcher-plants which had leaves
he shape of little jugs with lids. We
ally call them monkey pots. Why?)
cause," said Meor Din the know-all,"
n the little jugs are filled up with rain
er, the monkeys come and drink from
n."

As far as I can remember, the first time I ever stepped out of the kampung was to attend the wedding of a male relative of ours in a nearby kampung. My family and I were in the party that accompanied the groom to the Akad Nikah ceremony at the bride's house.

We went in two cars. The groom was driven in a new Morris Minor belonging to a teacher and we followed in the dresser's Austin.

Our party was very well received by the people at the bride's house although we arrived an hour late due to some reason or other. Bride-grooms never arrive on time, as I discovered in later years.

It was truly a big occasion and there was a huge crowd outside the house. As I entered I could tell, by the look of the handsomely built house and its furniture, that the girl was from a well-to-do family.

Waiting inside was the Kathi, other guests and witnesses.

There was no sigh of the bride because in this Akad Nikah ceremony only the groom was needed by the Kathi to sign the marriage papers.

Then came the tricky part. Watched by witnesses, the groom was asked to recite after the Kathi the holy words of matrimony in one breath. In my cousin's case, he had to do it three times because the witnesses weren't satisfied until the third time...
I JOIN YOU, MAT SOM BIN IBRAHIM, IN WEDLOCK TO SOFIAH BINTE OSMAN, WITH A DOWRY OF $22.50¢ CASH DOWN.
I TAKE SOFIAH BINTE OSMAN TO BE MY LAWFUL WEDDED WIF WITH THE DOWRY OF... ER... ER...

After that our party left with the groom for another house to rest. Everything had been arranged earlier for his temporary stay at the house.

At about 2 o'clock we returned to the girl's place for a big feast and most important of all for the Bersanding ceremony. They were made to sit on a platform.

Although this ceremony did not take long, they had to do it again that night when we were served with more food. But that was the last time we saw them for after the second Bersanding at about 8 p.m., the bride and the groom were ushered into their bedroom and left alone.

Suddenly things outside began to swing!
There was a loud happy tune with the Joget beat.
We rushed out. There was a band and dancing
girls!

This was really something. I had never seen
anything like this before. Probably those girls
were hired from a cabaret in Ipoh, a big town
30 miles away.

And they were ready! The band was playing.
All they needed now was for men folks to come
up to the stage (built temporarily for this
wedding) and dance with them! Anybody can
come up!

To my surprise it was dad who first went up!

The beat went on and in no time the stage was crowded with sporting men and their jovial partners doing the Joget. It's not difficult to do I guessed. Just move your feet and flap your wings.

They danced the night through. Dad was on the stage most of the time. On the whole it was a very happy occasion.

But later at home ... the atmosphere was not really good. Mum was in a bad mood because she didn't agree with his dancing about with the girls.

From inside my kelambu I could hear her saying angrily but softly: "A father of two doesn't dance with cabaret girls you know! That was only meant for bachelors! Next time you do that I'll go on stage — and pull you by the ears!"

Dad kept quiet.

At the age of nine, I began to feel that I was a responsible person. I had already started an extra class conducted by Tuan Syed where we learned how to pray. This picture shows Tuan Syed teaching us the Wudzu—a minor ritual ablution. It is the washing of face, hands and feet required before every prayer.

Oh! yes, by this time we already had another fellow in the family. My brother Abdul Rahman who as you can see enjoyed being taken for a ride on the spathe of the Pinang tree.

I was already able to do the shopping for provisions. Maimunah and Abdul Rahman used to follow me.

But most of the time I was missing from home because I would spend the whole day with the Meor brothers. My family would only see me at dinner time.

Dad and mum were not
in favour of this at all.
I knew about it all along
because many a night I became
the subject of their discussions.

Dad said I seemed only
to enjoy going out fishing
and playing around with the boys
and this would eventually
affect my studies.

What he said was true in a way.
I found going to school was a difficult task.
Especially getting up in the early hours of the
morning and going to the cold river for a bath.

Before going on my way
to school it was very important
for me to look at my fish trap.

And in school I was a quiet person.
I'd rather be by myself. Even during school recess I'd eat alone.
Some boys said I was a dreamer.

When the boys gathered to talk about fishing
I'd only listen from the back. I never participated.

However I was good in drawing. And I knew I was good because our teacher always picked my work to show the whole class as a good example.

But I was rather poor in arithmatic and my work was often shown as a bad example.

I can still recall
my first week in school too.
That was the time we were given
free powdered milk in a
Government health campaign.
We were encouraged to take
nutritional food.

For some of us it was the first time we tasted powdered milk.
We had a bit of stomach trouble.

On Friday and Saturday when the school was closed I would be with the boys all the time. On Friday morning we'd first go to help arrange the mats at the mosque for the Friday prayer. There'd be a big crowd later.

Pak Alang, the mosque caretaker, would give us yellow rice with beef curry in return for this little help.

After the Friday prayer
we'd go fishing naturally.

By this time I was already quite good at it. I already knew how to handle a catfish without giving it a chance to sting my fingers.

And sometimes we would go hand-fishing in the water. This was of course more darin

But this could be dangerous too because some fish — like the haruan — could be very aggressive when cornered.

Sometimes we'd borrow Pak Alang's sampan to go fishing with net.

We used to catch lobsters with the net.
And we were not bad at manning the sampan too...
even the one with a big hole could be put into use
—with the proper know-how.

If it was the fruit season, we'd spend more time guarding Meor Yusoff's durian trees.

Time travelled too fast I guessed. All of a sudden I was told that it was time for me to be circumcised. I was approaching ten years of age then. It was not something that I was happy to hear but I knew everyone had to pass through it.

It was my grandmother's wish that the Bersunat (circumcision) ceremony be held at her house. I was to be circumcised along with two other cousins of mine who were studying in a boarding school far away.

Grandma asked me to come along when she went around house to house announcing the occasion and inviting them to it.

"Yes that's the fellow," she'd say to her would-be-guests.

And so the big day came...
there was a big feast attended by a large crowd of
relatives and friends (in other words the whole kampung.)

The three of us were splendidly dressed in our
traditional costume. All the good food was placed before us.
But we just didn't feel like eating.

presents

The arrival of Tok Modin the circumcisor and his briefcase.

The Tok Modin was quite a funny fellow as we discovered after being introduced to him. We had a brief conversation since he asked a bit about ourselves, our studies, our favourite pastime.

"Have some chocolates," he said later and offered us some "chocolates" which were actually betel leaves and areca nuts.

(Earlier, he had uttered some magical formulae over the "chocolates" so that after chewing them we could undergo circumcision painlessly.)

Then out we went for a little procession to the river where we'd take a dip. We were greeted by the kampung "Rebana" team who accompanied us with Arabian songs.

I didn't know what the purpose of this short bath was. Whatever it was, I knew we were very special people that day. Even for this simple dip the guests — including women and girls — followed and watched us.

Then the moment came... the first chap (the eldest) was off to revisit Tok Modin. Good luck to him.

Then it was my turn...

It took place on a banana trunk.

In two minutes it was over! It was not very painful. Just like antbite!

The following two weeks was quite boring. We were not allowed to leave
the house because grandma was very strict. And what was worse she
only let us eat rice and salt fish... and drink boiled water.

However, after we had become well again, grandma gave us a treat a cinema show in Batu Gajah. My family came along too and dad bought the tickets.

Meanwhile the Meor brothers had gone in for a new past time ... dulang-washing. This method of finding tin using the pan was of course not right in the eyes of the law if you went panning at the back of a tin dredge! But the dredge people didn't seem to mind.

Furthermore what the folks worked was the waste — the mud and sand which was shot out through the back the dredge. But of course the mud contained some remnants of the mineral.

The Meor brothers invited me to joi them. I was thinking ... a kati of tin would fetch $5.25cts and some folk could get two katis per day ...

It didnt take long before I decided to join them.

Meor Din showed me how...

'rst collect the muddy sand into the pan.

with water added, the pan was gracefully rotated...

his let the light mud and sand out of the dulang...

HEE! HEE! HEE!

...leaving the heavy mineral behind.

I learnt fast.

But hard luck was upon us. The tin company management which for so long had faced this problem of preventing outsiders from coming to do illegal dulang washing had lost patience and complained to the police.

So one day Cpl. Mat Saman took action...

I retired early that night. My eyes were swollen because of that blow and probably excessive weeping. And I once again became the subject of discussion between my parents. This time my mother complained that father's punishment was too harsh.

"He was just trying to show you that he is able like the rest of the boys," she said.

"He should do well in his studies," said dad, "instead of stealing tin! His special examination is coming soon and he must pass in order to be admitted to the boarding school in Ipoh."

Anyway, a few days later my father took me to his 2-acre rubber plantation. I had no idea why he was taking me there. I had never been to this part before.

"You should know about this plantation," he said as we reached there after a long ride. My father's huge rubber trees were very old and the whole area was thick with undergrowth. All I knew about his plantation was that a fellow kampung folk was hired to tap the trees.

"Soon I'm planning to replant this land with high-yielding rubber. But first I have to get some people to clear it," he said.

Dad took out his parang and started cutting through shrubs in a particular spot and revealed a border stone.

He indicated the borders of his land and told me whose the neighbouring lands were.

"All right," he handed me the parang," now you clear the shrubs around the border stones so that we know our borders."

But I hesitated and said: "But father ... why not let the man who looks after this plantation take care of that?"

With my face turning red (from blush) I started clearing the undergrowth fast. I was confused too. Never had I thought my father would announce the inheritance that soon!

Obviously he was trying to make amends after that outburst of temper at the doorstep.

Dad added: "All this is of course on condition that you study well and pass your examination."

"All right, father."

The special examination that was approaching was for standard four pupils and several, including myself, were advised by our teacher to take it.

If I could pass I would be admitted to a high-standard boarding school in the big town of Ipoh. I would really be a somebody!

And so ... no more hanging around with the Meor brothers. I had to pass!

I passed.

It was hard to believe at first. The test papers were tough when I came to think of it (answers were given and all I had to do was tick the ones I thought correct.)

Our headmaster who was responsible for taking us to sit the examination in a big school in Kampar, broke the news to me one afternoon ... in front of his house.

"Along with three other fellows, you've passed."

I couldn't wait to tell everyone at home. Especially father.
But as I got back I saw him leaving in the land broker's motor-car.

Mother said all along she had known I would pass. When I asked where father had gone with the land broker she said: "They've gone to his plantation. It seems the tin company people are coming to inspect whether there's tin in the area. Many say there's a lot of tin there and if they buy the land it'll be quite a big sum.

"If they do buy your father's land we can use the money to get a home in the cheap housing scheme in Ipoh. Many local folks are thinking of the same.

"The tin company people are going to detect whether there's tin around here too," she said.

Weeks later, it was time for me to leave for the big school far away.
The Meor brothers came to send me off that morning.
Dad brought along a mattress (the hostel didn't supply mattresses.)

I was looking forward to my new life...

But it was about this time that I suddenly discovered
emotions I never knew I felt. I felt sad...

I still remember what my grandmother said
while waiting for the bus: "Listen... don't be arrogant there.
Be humble because we are humble people.
Always remember God and don't forget about us
    back here in the kampung."

It was as if I was going for good!

I couldn't describe my feelings as the bus took dad and me away. I couldn't tell for sure whether the town folks I was going to meet would know it when I mentioned the name of my kampung... it was so small... people were so few. But I loved it so much... it's river, its trees, the quiet houses and my friends.

And I sincerely hoped they wouldn't find more tin there because I want my kampung to go back to.